The Lord Hears Your Cries

Hope and Strength

from the Scriptures

in the Midst of

Domestic Violence

THE LORD HEARS YOUR CRIES

Hope and Strength
from the Scriptures
in the Midst of
Domestic Violence

CONTEMPORARY ENGLISH VERSION

ABS

AMERICAN BIBLE SOCIETY
NEW YORK

THE LORD HEARS YOUR CRIES

Contemporary English Version

This is a Portion of Holy Scripture in *Contemporary English Version*. The American Bible Society is a not-for-profit organization which publishes the Scriptures without doctrinal note or comment. Since 1816, its single mission has been to make the Word of God easily available to people everywhere at the lowest possible cost and in the languages they understand best. Working toward this goal, the ABS is a member of the United Bible Societies, a worldwide effort that extends to more than 180 countries and territories. You are urged to read the Bible and to share it with others. For a catalog of other Scripture, publications call 1-800-32-BIBLE, or write to the American Bible Society, 1865 Broadway, New York, NY 10023-7505. Visit the ABS website! www.americanbible.org.

Copyright © 1995, American Bible Society

Printed in the United States of America
Eng. Port. CEV560P-106023
ABS-9/98-32,500-34,500—LC1(2)

CONTENTS

A Message for You in Your Distress .. 6

Introduction 8

1. Shock and Disbelief:
   "You Say You Love Me,
   How Could You Hurt Me?" 10

2. Guilt and Pain:
   "Maybe If I Do More the Abuse
   Will Stop!" 14

3. Isolation and Fear:
   "What Will I Do Now?" 23

4. Anger and Resentment:
   "Stop Hurting Me!" 32

5. Depression and Low Self-Esteem:
   "I Feel So Depressed!" 42

6. Rebuilding Your Life:
   "I Will Put My Trust in the Lord!" .. 51

7. Acceptance and Peace:
   "I Will Praise the Lord!" 64

A Blessing for You... 68

Scripture Index 69

A MESSAGE FOR YOU IN YOUR DISTRESS

Dear Friend,

It is our sincere hope that the Scriptures in this booklet will bring you comfort during your distress. To help and guide you in your reading, we offer the following suggestions:

Begin with prayer. Ask God to comfort and strengthen you with the words from the Holy Scriptures.

Check the Contents page. Find the chapter that pertains to your feelings, and read the passages that express what you are feeling at the moment.

Reflect on the questions in the chapter you have read.

Allow yourself to release the emotions you are feeling — depression, anger, pain, fear, guilt, loneliness, self-pity, despair, sorrow, or any other emotion. Recognizing your feelings will help you to cope with them.

Conclude your reflection time with prayer, asking God to bless what you have read.

Copy Scripture verses or passages that have

special meaning to you and carry them with you. Reflect on them during the day.

Record on tape all your favorite Scripture from THE LORD HEARS YOUR CRIES, and listen to these verses in quiet moments. When you wake up in the morning, listen to the tape again, reflecting on the verses and asking God to be with you during the day.

Meet with others you trust to discuss what you are experiencing and what you believe God is saying to you in the Scripture readings.

Seek resources in your community that provide medical, legal and psychological help for yourself and other family members affected by the situation.

Be encouraged by this prayer to God for help:

Lord God,
You listen to the longings
of those who suffer.
You offer them hope,
and you pay attention
to their cries for help.

Psalm 10.17

THE LORD HEARS YOUR CRIES

Have you ever been hit or physically harmed by someone you love and trust? Have you had to endure the humiliation of abusive language and accusations? Do you live in fear because of threats made against you or others you love?

When someone you love is abusive, you may feel greatly confused. In your pain, you may experience many feelings — disbelief, shock, anger, guilt, fear. Opposing feelings can be present at the same time: perhaps anger and dependency, love and pain, and hurt with neediness. All these feelings are natural and must be sorted through.

Allow your feelings to be expressed in a safe place. By honestly evaluating all your feelings, whatever they are, you will be helped to find a solution to your situation that is right for you. Whatever the solution, the abuse must be stopped. Place your trust in God and allow the Lord to be your protector and to guide you into a place of safety.

Domestic violence is always potentially deadly, so the practical concerns you have for shelter, safety, intervention and treatment are vital. The issues that surface when domestic violence occurs are never purely religious or secular. It is important to avail yourself of both religious and secular sources of help. Use of medical, legal and psychological community resources is strongly encouraged to help you work out all the practical issues surrounding you when you attempt to rebuild your life. The community of faith and God's immeasurable help are just as critical when you try to understand the emotions evoked in you and the questions you naturally ask God when you experience such intense suffering. Seek out a cooperative harmony of effort between religious and secular sources of help to change your situation away from abuse, and help you to regain control over your life.

May God be your comfort as you take refuge in the words of Jesus, the apostle Paul, King David, Job, the prophets and the psalm writers. In the middle of their suffering, they all expressed their pain to God.

Jesus carried the heavy burden of the cross when he walked the road to his death. Jesus understands your suffering because he himself has suffered. As you place your trust in him, he promises to lift your heavy burden and to make it light. He will always be your rest as you come to rest in him, for he gave his life because of his love for you.

If you are tired from carrying heavy burdens, come to me and I will give you rest. Take the yoke I give you. Put it on your shoulders and learn from me. I am gentle and humble, and you will find rest. This yoke is easy to bear, and this burden is light.

Matthew 11.28-30

Shock and Disbelief

"You Say You Love Me,
How Could You Hurt Me?"

When someone you love hurts you and is abusive, you may feel shock. Denying the reality of the abuse and making excuses for the abuser are common reactions. You may try to deny the violence by asking, "I can't believe it, how could this happen?" God understands your confusion. The Lord knows the grief you face when your trust has been betrayed through violence.

**But it was my closest friend,
the one I trusted most.**

Listen, God, to my prayer!
    Don't reject my request.
Please listen and help me.
My thoughts are troubled,
    and I keep groaning
because my loud enemies
    shout and attack.
They treat me terribly
    and hold angry grudges.
My heart is racing fast,
    and I am afraid of dying.
I am trembling with fear,
    completely terrified.

I wish I had wings
    like a dove,

so I could fly far away
    and be at peace.
I would go and live
    in some distant desert.
I would quickly find shelter
from howling winds
    and raging storms.

•••

My enemies are not the ones
    who sneer and make fun.
I could put up with that
    or even hide from them.
But it was my closest friend,
    the one I trusted most.

•••

My friend turned against me
    and broke his promise.
His words were smoother
than butter, and softer
    than olive oil.

Psalm 55. 1-8, 12, 13, 20, 21a

Jesus understands your misery.

Jesus, the faithful son of God, also suffered bitterly from betrayal. Judas Iscariot, his friend and disciple, betrayed him with a kiss. After Jesus was arrested, he was mocked, spat upon, tortured and nailed to a cross.

He was betrayed.

Jesus was still speaking, when Judas the betrayer came up. He was one of the twelve disciples, and a mob of men armed with swords and clubs were with him. They had been sent by the chief priests, the nation's leaders, and the teachers of the Law of Moses. Judas had told them ahead of time, "Arrest the man I greet with a kiss. Tie him up tight and lead him away."

Judas walked right up to Jesus and said, "Teacher!" Then Judas kissed him, and the men grabbed Jesus and arrested him.

Mark 14. 43-46

He was mocked.

The soldiers led Jesus inside the courtyard of the fortress and called together the rest of the troops. They put a purple robe on him, and on his head they placed a crown that they had made out of thorn branches. They made fun of Jesus and shouted, "Hey, you king of the Jews!" Then they beat him on the head with a stick. They spit on him and knelt down and pretended to worship him.

When the soldiers had finished making fun of Jesus, they took off the purple robe. They put his own clothes back on him and led him off to be nailed to a cross.

Mark 15. 16-20

Pause and ask yourself...

Do I feel numb? Am I denying my feelings? Am I afraid to face my feelings? Do I feel as if my trust is broken? Do I feel betrayed? Am I able to feel God's presence in the middle of my feelings?

After suffering abuse, you may feel as if your faith in people and God has been damaged. God can reestablish a healthy sense of trust: trust that even though certain people have let you down, not everyone will, and ultimately God can always be trusted.

I trust in you, Lord.

But I trust you, LORD,
 and I claim you as my God.
My life is in your hands.
Save me from enemies
 who hunt me down.
Smile on me, your servant.
 Have pity and rescue me.

Psalm 31. 14-16

Please keep me safe, Lord.

I offer you my heart, LORD God,
 and I trust you.
Don't make me ashamed
 or let enemies defeat me.
Don't disappoint any
 of your worshipers,
but disappoint all
 deceitful liars.
Show me your paths
 and teach me to follow;
guide me by your truth
 and instruct me.
You keep me safe,
 and I always trust you.

Psalm 25. 1-5

Guilt and Pain

"Maybe If I Do More The Abuse Will Stop!"

The torment of being violently assaulted by the person you love can cause you to have feelings of guilt, even though you are not at fault. You may feel guilty, as if you brought the violence upon yourself. You may be saying to yourself: "if only I was a better person", "if only I had done more to please".

However, you are not to blame. You are not responsible for causing your loved one to abuse you. Abuse is always a choice made by the abuser. No one has the right to violate you with violence.

You are precious to God.

All of you surely know that you are God's temple and that his Spirit lives in you. Together you are God's holy temple, and God will destroy anyone who destroys his temple.

> 1 Corinthians 3. 16, 17

You are spotless.

You may take on a burden of feeling unworthy and unclean when the batterer treats you with contempt and abuse. God however sees you as worthy and clean.

You were rescued by the precious blood of Christ, that spotless and innocent lamb. Christ was chosen even before the world was created, but because of you, he did not come until these last days. And when he did come, it was to lead you to have faith in God, who raised him from death and honored him in a glorious way. That's why you have put your faith and hope in God.

You obeyed the truth, and your souls were made pure.

1 Peter 1. 19-22a

You are chosen by God.

Praise the God and Father of our Lord Jesus Christ for the spiritual blessings that Christ has brought us from heaven! Before the world was created, God had Christ choose us to live with him and to be his holy and innocent and loving people. God was kind and decided that Christ would choose us to be God's own adopted children. God was very kind to us because of the Son he dearly loves, and so we should praise God.

Christ sacrificed his life's blood to set us free, which means that our sins are now forgiven. Christ did this because God was so kind to us. God has great wisdom and understanding, and by what Christ has done, God has shown us his own mysterious ways. Then when the time is right, God will do all that he has planned, and Christ will bring together everything in heaven and on earth.

Ephesians 1. 3-10

Pause and ask yourself...

Do I feel guilty or worthless? Do I feel that I am to blame, that I can't seem to please others no matter how hard I try? How do I feel about God? Can I turn to God in my pain?

God is fair and loving.

The question of who suffers and why must not be trivialized with easy explanations; a person's suffering does not demonstrate guilt. Also, trying to live a virtuous life does not protect a person from being sinned against. God is not punishing you; the responsibility for your suffering at the hands of the abuser must be squarely placed where it belongs: on the abuser. Your abuse is the sin of the abuser.

The Bible contains examples of innocent people who suffered. Job was a moral man who suffered. Job's friend Elihu knew that Job was a blameless man. He understood Job's frustration with his prolonged misery. Even though Job was suffering, Elihu knew that God is a fair and loving God. Job could always trust God to be with him and help him in the middle of his suffering.

Elihu said to Job:
> I have something else to say
>   in God's defense.
> God always does right —
> and this knowledge
>   comes straight from God.
> You can rest assured
>   that what I say is true.
> Although God is mighty,
> he cares about everyone
>   and makes fair decisions.
>
> The wicked are cut down,
> and those who are wronged
>   receive justice.

Job 36. 2b-6

Sometimes other people will think that when someone suffers, the suffering indicates that the person has sinned and is being punished by God. Similarly, people asked Jesus why a blind man was born blind, "Is this man being punished or are his parents?" Jesus denied that God was punishing either the blind man or his parents. He declared that God was using the healing of the man's blindness to display God's glory. The abuse you are enduring does not mean that God is punishing you for a sin you have committed.

As Jesus walked along, he saw a man who had been blind since birth. Jesus' disciples asked, "Teacher, why was this man born blind? Was it because he or his parents sinned?"

"No, it wasn't!" Jesus answered. "But because of his blindness, you will see God work a miracle for him. As long as it is day, we must do what the one who sent me wants me to do. When night comes, no one can work. While I am in the world, I am the light for the world."

After Jesus said this, he spit on the ground. He made some mud and smeared it on the man's eyes. Then he said, "Go and wash off the mud in Siloam Pool." The man went and washed in Siloam, which means "One Who Is Sent." When he had washed off the mud, he could see.

John 9. 1-7

You may not think God is punishing you, but may ask, "Why is God allowing me to be mistreated? Why is my abuser allowed to keep abusing me?" The general question of why God allows suffering is complicated; there are no easy answers. Job also asked God similar questions.

> Why is life so hard?
> Why do we suffer?
> We are slaves in search of shade;
> we are laborers longing
> for our wages.
> God has made my days drag on
> and my nights miserable.
> I pray for night to end,
> but it stretches out
> while I toss and turn.
> My parched skin is covered
> with worms, dirt, and sores,
> and my days are running out
> quicker than the thread
> of a fast-moving needle.
>
> • • •
>
> And so, I cry out to you
> in agony and distress.
>
> Job 7. 1-6, 11

Pause and ask yourself...

Do I feel like Job? Do I see the person who abuses me as blaming me for things that I have not done? How does that person take their frustrations out on me? Do I then feel guilty for things I have not done? Do others believe I brought the abuse upon myself? Do others take the side of the person who abuses me? Do others believe that God is punishing me? Do I believe that God is punishing me?

The Lord hears you in your pain.

In your exhaustion you also may ask God, "How long must I endure this terrible suffering?" In your anguish you may feel that God does not hear or care about you. God does care and promises to always be with you in a loving way during your suffering.

> How much longer, LORD,
>   will you forget about me?
> Will it be forever?
>   How long will you hide?
> How long must I be confused
>   and miserable all day?
> How long will my enemies
>   keep beating me down?
>
> Please listen, LORD God,
>   and answer my prayers.
> Make my eyes sparkle again,
> or else I will fall
>   into the sleep of death.
> My enemies will say,
>   "Now we've won!"
> They will be greatly pleased
>   when I am defeated.
>
> I trust your love,
> and I feel like celebrating
>   because you rescued me.
> You have been good to me, LORD,
>   and I will sing about you.

Psalm 13

Pause and ask yourself...

Can I believe that God hears me in my pain? Can I give all my pain and guilty feeling over to God?

God wants to free you from injustice.

Jesus was sent by God to offer freedom to everyone who suffers.

Jesus went back to Nazareth, where he had been brought up, and as usual he went to the meeting place on the Sabbath. When he stood up to read from the Scriptures, he was given the book of Isaiah the prophet. He opened it and read,

> "The Lord's Spirit
>   has come to me,
> because he has chosen me
> to tell the good news
>   to the poor.
> The Lord has sent me
> to announce freedom
>   for prisoners,
> to give sight to the blind,
> to free everyone
>   who suffers,
> and to say, 'This is the year
>   the Lord has chosen.'"

Jesus closed the book, then handed it back to the man in charge and sat down. Everyone in the meeting place looked straight at Jesus.

Then Jesus said to them, "What you have just heard me read has come true today."

Luke 4. 16-21

God wants you to choose life.

As God delivered the Israelites from slavery in Egypt and brought them into the promised land of Israel, God wants to deliver you from the captivity of violence. God desires you to be liberated from oppression.

Moses said to Israel:

You know God's laws, and it isn't impossible to obey them. His commands aren't in heaven, so you can't excuse yourselves by saying, "How can we obey the Lord's commands? They are in heaven, and no one can go up to get them, then bring them down and explain them to us." And you can't say, "How can we obey the Lord's commands? They are across the sea, and someone must go across, then bring them back and explain them to us." No, these commands are nearby and you know them by heart. All you have to do is obey!

Today I am giving you a choice. You can choose life and success or death and disaster. I am commanding you to be loyal to the Lord, to live the way he has told you, and to obey his laws and teachings. You are about to cross the Jordan River and take the land that he is giving you. If you obey him, you will live and become successful and powerful.

• • •

Choose life! Be completely faithful to the Lord your God, love him, and do whatever he tells you. The Lord is the only one who can give life, and he will let you live a long time in the land that he promised to your ancestors Abraham, Isaac, and Jacob.

Deuteronomy 30. 11-17, 19b, 20

Jesus has come to break you away from your oppression and bring you into abundant life.

Jesus said:

I tell you for certain that I am the gate for the sheep. Everyone who came before me was a thief or a robber, and the sheep did not listen to any of them. I am the gate. All

who come in through me will be saved.
Through me they will come and go and find pasture.

A thief comes only to rob, kill, and destroy. I came so that everyone would have life, and have it in its fullest.

John 10. 7-10

God is always ready to help you.

God is our mighty fortress,
always ready to help
   in times of trouble.
And so, we won't be afraid!
   Let the earth tremble
and the mountains tumble
   into the deepest sea.
Let the ocean roar and foam,
and its raging waves
   shake the mountains.

A river and its streams
   bring joy to the city,
which is the sacred home
   of God Most High.
God is in that city,
and it won't be shaken.
   He will help it at dawn.

Nations rage! Kingdoms fall!
But at the voice of God
   the earth itself melts.
The LORD All-Powerful
   is with us.

Psalm 46. 1-7a

Isolation and Fear

"What Will I Do Now?"

The abuse you are experiencing may cut you off from friends and relatives. You may feel shame and humiliation at being abused and may hide your pain from others. The abuser may try to control you by keeping you away from other people, or may threaten to hurt you if you tell anyone what is happening. You may feel terrible loneliness and fear. In your isolation you may fear that God has rejected and abandoned you. You may be asking, "Where is God?"

God will comfort you in your distress, and will answer your prayers. The Lord promises to always be with you in times of trouble. Even though you may feel alone and afraid, God is with you.

God will never leave you.

> I pray to you, Lord God,
>   and I beg you to listen.
> In days filled with trouble,
>   I search for you.
> And at night I tirelessly
> lift my hands in prayer,
>   refusing comfort.
> When I think of you,
>   I feel restless and weak.

Because of you, LORD God,
    I can't sleep.
I am restless
    and can't even talk.

•••

Each night my mind
    is flooded with questions:
"Have you rejected me forever?
    Won't you be kind again?
Is this the end of your love
    and your promises?
Have you forgotten
    how to have pity?
Do you refuse to show mercy
    because of your anger?"

•••

Our LORD, I will remember
the things you have done,
    your miracles of long ago.
I will think about each one
    of your mighty deeds.
Everything you do is right,
and no other god
    compares with you.
You alone work miracles,
and you have let nations
    see your mighty power.

Psalm 77. 1-4, 6-9, 11-14

The Lord knows your isolation and pain.

Jesus felt abandoned by God when he was dying on the cross.

At noon the sky turned dark and stayed that way until three o'clock. Then about that time Jesus shouted, "Eli, Eli, lema sabachthani?" which means, "My God, my God, why have you deserted me?"

Matthew 27. 45, 46

Just as Jesus in his pain on the cross cried out the words of the psalm writer, you may feel that God has abandoned you and that people have deserted you. Jesus understands.

> My God, my God, why have you
>   deserted me?
> Why are you so far away?
> Won't you listen to my groans
>   and come to my rescue?
> I cry out day and night,
> but you don't answer,
>   and I can never rest.
>
> Psalm 22. 1, 2

Pause and ask yourself...

Do I feel that God has rejected and abandoned me? Do I feel cut off from God and others? How does this make me feel? How can I counteract these feeling?

Sometimes no one will believe that you are being abused. You may even be blamed for provoking the abuser to violence. Although no one may believe you, God knows your situation well. God knows your heart and the heart of the person hurting you. You are never alone with God in your heart because God really cares. In your time of trial the Lord will lead you through the deepest darkness.

The Lord will keep you safe.

> You, LORD, are the light
>   that keeps me safe.
> I am not afraid of anyone.
> You protect me,
>   and I have no fears.

Brutal people may attack
and try to kill me,
> but they will stumble.
Fierce enemies may attack,
> but they will fall.
Armies may surround me,
> but I won't be afraid;
war may break out,
> but I will trust you.

• • •

Please listen when I pray!
> Have pity. Answer my prayer.
My heart tells me to pray.
I am eager to see your face,
> so don't hide from me.
I am your servant,
and you have helped me
> Don't turn from me in anger.
You alone keep me safe.
> Don't reject or desert me.

Psalm 27. 1-3, 7-9

The Lord is with you.

You, LORD, are my shepherd.
> I will never be in need.
You let me rest in fields
of green grass.
You lead me to streams
of peaceful water,
> and you refresh my life.

You are true to your name,
and you lead me
> along the right paths.
I may walk through valleys
as dark as death,
> but I won't be afraid.
You are with me,

and your shepherd's rod
> makes me feel safe.

You treat me to a feast,
> while my enemies watch.
You honor me as your guest,
and you fill my cup
> until it overflows.
Your kindness and love
will always be with me
> each day of my life,
and I will live forever
> in your house, LORD.

Psalm 23

Pause and ask yourself...

Do I feel that God doesn't care? Can I think of ways in which God has looked out for me? How might God be present to me through others' efforts to assist me?

Isaiah, the prophet, pleaded with God to deliver Israel from exile. In your pain you may feel cut off from God and exiled from every loving relationship. But, God's love is close and real. The Lord created you and will be with you in all your trials. You are never alone with God by your side, for you belong to the Lord, your creator. God cares for you in a way that is stronger than the love of a mother for her young.

You are never cut off from God.

> Don't be afraid. I am with you.
> Don't tremble with fear.
> > I am your God.
> I will make you strong,
> as I protect you with my arm
> > and give you victories.

Everyone who hates you
> will be terribly disgraced;
those who attack
> will vanish into thin air.
You will look around
> for those brutal enemies,
but you won't find them
> because they will be gone.

I am the LORD your God.
I am holding your hand,
> so don't be afraid.
I am here to help you.

> Isaiah 41. 10-13

You belong to the Lord.

Descendants of Jacob,
I, the LORD, created you
> and formed your nation.
Israel, don't be afraid.
> I have rescued you.
I have called you by name;
> now you belong to me.
When you cross deep rivers,
I will be with you,
> and you won't drown.
When you walk through fire,
you won't be burned
> or scorched by the flames.

I am the LORD, your God,
the Holy One of Israel,
> the God who saves you.

> Isaiah 43. 1-3a

The Lord will never forget you.

The LORD answered,
"Could a mother forget a child
> who nurses at her breast?

> Could she fail to love an infant
>   who came from her own body?
> Even if a mother could forget,
>   I will never forget you.

Isaiah 49.15

Pause and ask yourself...

How do I describe God's love for me? Do I see God as a loving father or as a protective mother? Can I appreciate God as the most loyal of friends?

The Lord knew you in your mother's womb, and knows all your pain and sorrow. The Lord is intimately aware of all your emotions: nothing is hidden from God. You may be rejected by certain people but you will not be rejected by God. Nothing can separate you from God's love.

The Lord is nearby.

> You have looked deep
> into my heart, LORD,
>   and you know all about me.
> You know when I am resting
>   or when I am working,
> and from heaven
>   you discover my thoughts.
>
> You notice everything I do
>   and everywhere I go.
> Before I even speak a word,
>   you know what I will say,
> and with your powerful arm
> you protect me
>   from every side.
> I can't understand all of this!
> Such wonderful knowledge
>   is far above me.

Where could I go to escape
from your Spirit
    or from your sight?
If I were to climb up
to the highest heavens,
    you would be there.
If I were to dig down
to the world of the dead
    you would also be there.

Suppose I had wings
like the dawning day
    and flew across the ocean.
Even then your powerful arm
    would guide and protect me.
Or suppose I said, "I'll hide
in the dark until night comes
    to cover me over."
But you see in the dark
because daylight and dark
    are all the same to you.

You are the one
who put me together
    inside my mother's body,
and I praise you because of
the wonderful way
    you created me.
Everything you do is marvelous!
    Of this I have no doubt.

Nothing about me
    is hidden from you!
I was secretly woven together
    deep in the earth below,
but with your own eyes you saw
    my body being formed.
Even before I was born,
you had written in your book
    everything I would do.

> Your thoughts are far beyond
> my understanding,
> much more than I
> could ever imagine.
> I try to count your thoughts,
> but they outnumber the grains
> of sand on the beach.
> And when I awake,
> I will find you nearby.

Psalm 139. 1-18

Not only is God's love greater than the love of a gentle mother for her young, and impossible to escape, but it is built on justice and fairness. The LORD will deal in justice with the violence you are experiencing. God promises to deal with your abuser and to eventually lead you to the proper solution.

The Lord brings justice!

> The heavens announce,
> "The LORD brings justice!"
> Everyone sees God's glory.
>
> Love the LORD
> and hate evil!
> God protects his loyal people
> and rescues them
> from violence.

Psalm 97. 6, 10

Pause and ask yourself...

How can I reach out to the support system available to me? How is God working justice through the people who are there to help me?

Anger and Resentment

"Stop Hurting Me!"

Anger and resentment are natural outcomes of being abused. God, in whose image you are created, instilled within you these natural emotions to help you to survive. God understands your anger at the evil of abuse. Anger can be a gift which will motivate you toward finding positive ways to reclaim your power. Anger can strengthen you to do the things that need to be done. It can give you the strength to begin to change your situation. However, the Lord wants you to express these emotions in a healthy and constructive manner. The most effective use of your anger will help lead you to reclaim your life from abuse.

God directs anger against evil.

God is holy, so God's anger is moral outrage that opposes people's sin, unbelief, error, disobedience and idolatry. Jesus expressed disapproval when unbelievers tried to prevent him from doing good by healing a woman on the Sabbath.

One Sabbath, Jesus was teaching in a Jewish meeting place, and a woman was there who had been crippled by an evil spirit for eighteen years. She was completely bent over and could not straighten up. When Jesus saw the woman, he called her over and said, "You are now well." He placed his hands on her, and right away she stood up straight and praised God.

The man in charge of the meeting place was angry because Jesus had healed someone on the Sabbath. So he said to the people, "Each week has six days when we can work. Come and be healed on one of those days, but not on the Sabbath."

The Lord replied, "Are you trying to fool someone? Won't any one of you untie your ox or donkey and lead it out to drink on a Sabbath? This woman belongs to the family of Abraham, but Satan has kept her bound for eighteen years. Isn't it right to set her free on the Sabbath?" Jesus' words made his enemies ashamed. But everyone else in the crowd was happy about the wonderful things he was doing.

Luke 13. 10-17

Jesus was angry at the moneychangers in the temple who were corrupting the Lord's place of worship. Jesus sought to stop the corruption of that which is sacred.

After Jesus and his disciples reached Jerusalem, he went into the temple and began chasing out everyone who was selling and buying. He turned over the tables of the moneychangers and the benches of those who were selling doves. Jesus would not let anyone carry things through the temple. Then he taught the people and said, "The Scriptures say, 'My house should be called a place of worship for all nations.' But you have made it a place where robbers hide!"

The chief priests and the teachers of the Law of Moses heard what Jesus said, and they started looking for a way to kill him. They were afraid of him, because the crowds were completely amazed at his teaching.

Mark 11. 15-18

God opposes the evil of abuse.

You are God's Holy temple, and God does not want you to be violated and hurt. Your body is the dwelling place of God and is not to be dishonored or abused by anyone.

You surely know that your body is a temple where the Holy Spirit lives. The Spirit is in you and is a gift from God. You are no longer your own. God paid a great price for you. So use your body to honor God.

1 Corinthians 6. 19,20

God wants you to love yourself as well as you love God and your neighbor.

One of the teachers of the Law of Moses came up while Jesus and the Sadducees were arguing. When he heard Jesus give a good answer, he asked him, "What is the most important commandment?"

Jesus answered, "The most important one says: 'People of Israel, you have only one Lord and God. You must love him with all your heart, soul, mind, and strength.' The second most important commandment says: 'Love others as much as you love yourself.' No other commandment is more important than these."

The man replied, "Teacher, you are certainly right to say there is only one God. It is also true that we must love God with all our heart, mind, and strength, and that we must love others as much as we love ourselves. These commandments are more important than all the sacrifices and offerings that we could possibly make."

When Jesus saw that the man had given a sensible answer, he told him, "You are not far from

God's kingdom." After this, no one dared ask Jesus any more questions.

Mark 12. 28-34

God opposes violence.

Because someone you love is using violence to control and manipulate you, you may feel that God is angry with you. The Lord is only angry with injustice. God sees you with loving kindness and sympathy. God recognizes that the violence done to you is wrong and holds the abuser responsible for it.

You, Lord God,
    are my protector.
Rescue me and keep me safe
    from all who chase me.
Or else they will rip me apart
like lions attacking a victim,
    and no one will save me.

I am innocent, Lord God!
I have not betrayed a friend
    or had pity on an enemy
    who attacks for no reason.

• • •

Get angry, Lord God!
    Do something!
Attack my furious enemies.
    See that justice is done.

• • •

Our Lord, judge the nations!
Judge me and show that I
    am honest and innocent.
You know every heart and mind,
    and you always do right.
Now make violent people stop,
but protect all of us
    who obey you.

You, God, are my shield,
the protector of everyone
    whose heart is right.
You see that justice is done,
and each day
    you take revenge.

Psalm 7. 1-4, 6, 8-11

You may be angry with God and believe that God is uncaringly allowing the abuse to go on. Sometimes evil people prosper, in a way that is beyond your understanding. God sees your suffering and understands your questioning.

Why do evil people live so long
    and gain such power?

• • •

They have no worries at home,
    and God never punishes them.

• • •

Those who are evil say
    to God All-Powerful,
"Leave us alone! Don't bother us
    with your teachings.
What do we gain from praying
    and worshiping you?
We succeeded all on our own."
And so, I keep away from them
    and their evil schemes.

Job 21. 7, 9, 14-16

Pause and ask yourself...

How do I feel controlled and manipulated by the violence? How do I feel when people who do wrong sometimes seem to prosper? Do

I feel that God is allowing these people to keep hurting others? Is anger with God making me feel distant from God or from other loving relationships that can support me? Do I feel angry at God for allowing the violence to go on?

Healthy anger is a gift.

The anger you feel is God's weapon, built into you biologically, to help you defend your personal integrity and boundaries. Naturally, you are very angry: not only at the abuse but also honestly with the person who abuses you. God understands your intense anger. Even the psalm writers expressed deep anger at cruelty.

> How I wish that you would kill
> all cruel and heartless people
>   and protect me from them!
> They are always rebelling
>   and speaking evil of you.
> You know I hate anyone
> who hates you, LORD,
>   and refuses to obey.
> They are my enemies too,
>   and I truly hate them.
>
> Look deep into my heart, God,
> and find out everything
>   I am thinking.
> Don't let me follow evil ways,
> but lead me in the way
>   that time has proven true.
>
> Psalm 139. 19-24

Use your anger to seek justice.

Anger can strengthen you with the energy necessary to effectively change your life. Let your anger fuel activity and be an incentive to new growth. Jesus teaches that perseverance in prayer, and in actively working toward justice for yourself, is rewarded. God blesses anger that insists on seeking justice. This is a way to process your anger constructively, and a way to find courage when you are afraid your anger will overwhelm you.

Jesus told his disciples a story about how they should keep on praying and never give up:

In a town there was once a judge who didn't fear God or care about people. In that same town there was a widow who kept going to the judge and saying, "Make sure that I get fair treatment in court."

For a while the judge refused to do anything. Finally, he said to himself, "Even though I don't fear God or care about people, I will help this widow because she keeps on bothering me. If I don't help her, she will wear me out."

The Lord said:

Think about what that crooked judge said. Won't God protect his chosen ones who pray to him day and night? Won't he be concerned for them? He will surely hurry and help them. But when the Son of Man comes, will he find on this earth anyone with faith?

Luke 18. 1-8

Pause and ask yourself...

Am I able to feel my anger or am I repressing and denying it? Am I afraid that my anger will overwhelm me and others if expressed? Does my anger come out against even more powerless members of my family? How can I express my anger in a constructive and healthy manner? How can I honestly express my anger to God?

God and others can help you process your anger appropriately.

God does not want you to swallow or deny your anger: it is normal to be angry with someone who abuses you. Hastily getting rid of your anger and forgiving before you are ready merely covers over a boiling rage. Connecting with your anger is often the way God will strengthen you to act on your own behalf. It is vital, however, that when you are able to acknowledge your anger that you are able to express it in a safe way. God does not want you to needlessly risk your health or life. The Lord wants you to be protected from harm.

> You see everything, LORD!
> Please don't keep silent
>   or stay so far away.
> Fight to defend me, Lord God,
> and prove that I am right
>   by your standards.
> Don't let them laugh at me
>   or say to each other,
> "Now we've got what we want!
>   We'll gobble him down!"
>
> Disappoint and confuse
> all who are glad
>   to see me in trouble,
> but disgrace and embarrass
> my proud enemies who say to me,
>   "You are nothing!"
>
> Let all who want me to win
>   be happy and joyful.

> From now on let them say,
> > "The LORD is wonderful!
> God is glad when all goes well
> > for his servant."
> Then I will shout all day,
> > "Praise the LORD God!
> > He did what was right."

Psalm 35. 22-28

As a balance to expressing your anger, the Lord, cautions people about the dangers of unholy anger. Taking revenge is in God's hands. For although people's anger may be moral and may be directed against injustice and evil, it may be mixed with destructive hatred and rage. God asks people to be slow to anger, and not to sin when angry.

The apostle Paul said:
Dear friends, don't try to get even. Let God take revenge. In the Scriptures the Lord says,

> "I am the one to take revenge
> and pay them back."

Romans 12. 19

With the aid of prayer, God can help you to sort out your feelings and help you to find the proper actions to take. When Jesus' disciples asked him how to pray Jesus said.

You should pray like this:

> Our Father in heaven,
> help us to honor
> > your name.
> Come and set up
> > your kingdom,

so that everyone on earth
  will obey you,
as you are obeyed
  in heaven.
Give us our food for today.
Forgive us for doing wrong,
  as we forgive others.
Keep us from being tempted
  and protect us from evil.

Matthew 6. 9-13

For all who are mistreated, the Lord brings justice.

God's understanding is total. The Lord can deal with the heart of the person who abuses you, and help you to have peace in your heart. In the end, the Lord will bring justice.

For all who are mistreated,
  the LORD brings justice.
He taught his Law to Moses
and showed all Israel
  what he could do.

The LORD is merciful!
He is kind and patient,
  and his love never fails.

•••

How great is God's love for all
  who worship him?
Greater than the distance
  between heaven and earth!
How far has the LORD taken
  our sins from us?
Farther than the distance
  from east to west!

Psalm 103. 6-8, 11, 12

Depression and Low Self-Esteem

"I Feel So Depressed!"

You may feel an enormous sense of depression. The loss of intimacy caused by abuse can make you feel dejected. The trauma of repeated battering can eliminate your self-esteem and destroy your feelings of self-worth. You may be mourning the loss of a happy home life and the destruction of a love relationship that is important to you. You may feel loss of hope. In your despair you may feel that things in your life will never be good again.

I tell myself, "I am finished!..."

I tell myself, "I am finished!
I can't count on the LORD
   to do anything for me."
Just thinking of my troubles
and my lonely wandering
   makes me miserable.
That's all I ever think about,
   and I am depressed."

Lamentations 3. 18-20

Pause and ask yourself...

Do I feel depression or a loss of hope? How has the battering reduced my sense of self-worth?

The Lord knows your deep despair. You may feel that your depression will never end. For as the psalmist writes,

Day and night my tears are my only food...

> As a deer gets thirsty
>   for streams of water,
> I truly am thirsty
>   for you, my God.
> In my heart, I am thirsty
> for you, the living God.
>   When will I see your face?
> Day and night my tears
>   are my only food,
> as everyone keeps asking,
>   "Where is your God?"

Psalm 42. 1-3

Pause and ask yourself...

Does my life feel empty and without love? Does my depression feel endless, as if it will never stop? How do I feel about God when I'm depressed?

The results of repeated trauma can be extremely destructive, not only to your emotional well-being, but to your physical well-being. You may have overcome repeated assaults or even have escaped death. Others may not know or understand that you face the possibility of death and injury every day. You may feel physically exhausted and emotionally drained, which can add to your depression. As the psalmist writes,

I am worn out and weak, moaning and in distress.

My body is twisted and bent,
 and I groan all day long.
Fever has my back in flames,
 and I hurt all over.
I am worn out and weak,
 moaning and in distress.

You, Lord, know every one
 of my deepest desires,
and my noisy groans
 are no secret to you.
My heart is beating fast.
I feel weak all over,
 and my eyes are red.

Psalm 38. 6-10

Pause and ask yourself...

Do I feel physically exhausted or sick? Do I feel emotionally drained? Is my depression caused partly from exhaustion? Can I find a place of safety and comfort in order to heal?

No one may recognize the extent of the abuse that you are enduring, which can cause great depression. You may have escaped injury or death, and still be in danger. As the psalmist expressed,

...you have rescued me from the chains of death.

Death attacked from all sides,
and I was captured
 by its painful chains.

But when I was really hurting,
I prayed and said, "LORD,
    please don't let me die!"

•••

You, LORD, have saved
    my life from death,
    my eyes from tears,
    my feet from stumbling.
Now I will walk at your side
    in this land of the living.
I was faithful to you
    when I was suffering,
though in my confusion I said,
    "I can't trust anyone!"

•••

You are deeply concerned
when one of your loyal people
    faces death.

I worship you, LORD,
    just as my mother did,
and you have rescued me
    from the chains of death.

Psalm 116. 3, 4, 8-11, 15, 16

Pause and ask yourself...

Have I been rescued from death? Is my life in danger now? How might I or others help relieve my depression and help me to get myself out of danger?

You may feel as if you have died emotionally from being continually beaten and fearful. You may have cut off all emotion in order not to feel pain, and may have numbed yourself as a defense against feeling anything. While this numbness can be helpful in defending yourself against the pain of abuse, you need to guard against permanently cutting yourself off from all emotion. Feeling emotion again will help energize you to free yourself from a potentially deadly situation. God understands and sympathizes with the emotional numbness you feel. Try not to cut yourself off from life. In your emotions resides the warmth of your life!

I have given up all hope, and I feel numb all over.

I have given up all hope,
    and I feel numb all over.

I remember to think about
the many things you did
    in years gone by.
Then I lift my hands in prayer,
because my soul is a desert,
    thirsty for water from you.

Please hurry, LORD,
and answer my prayer.
    I feel hopeless.
Don't turn away
    and leave me here to die.
Each morning let me learn
more about your love
    because I trust you.
I come to you in prayer,
    asking for your guidance.

Psalm 143. 4-8

Pause and ask yourself...

Do I feel nothing or is my life in shades of gray? Do I feel numb? Do I have the energy to feel again? How can God and others help to give me the strength to feel, so I can go on to new life?

Send your light and your truth to guide me.

You may feel sad, because depression can mask any unprocessed and overwhelming emotion. You may even feel guilt for being depressed. Depression can be the symptom of any deep painful emotion you have not dealt with.

> Show that I am right, God!
> Defend me against everyone
>   who doesn't know you;
> rescue me from each
>   of those deceitful liars.
> I run to you
>   for protection.
> Why have you turned me away?
> Why must enemies mistreat me
>   and make me sad?
>
> Send your light and your truth
>   to guide me.
> Let them lead me to your house
>   on your sacred mountain.
> Then I will worship
> at your altar because you
>   make me joyful.
> You are my God,
>   and I will praise you.
> Yes, I will praise you
>   as I play my harp.
>
> Why am I discouraged?
> Why am I restless?
>   I trust you!
> And I will praise you again
> because you help me,
>   and you are my God.

Psalm 43

Save me, Lord God!

Another danger of depression is that it can paralyze you, and keep you from using healthy coping emotions that will enable you to deal with the abusive situation. Coming to grips with the emotions, that are covered over by depression, can give you the emotional energy necessary to deal with the abuser and to pursue a healthy life. Seek out the help God wants to provide from the community resources at your disposal. God wants you to be stimulated to act on your behalf.

> Save me, LORD God!
>   Hurry and help.
> Disappoint and confuse
>   all who want to kill me.
> Turn away and disgrace
>   all who want to hurt me.
> Embarrass and shame those
>   who say, "We told you so!"
>
> Let your worshipers celebrate
>   and be glad because of you.
> They love your saving power,
> so let them always say,
>   "God is wonderful!"
> I am poor and needy,
> but you, the LORD God,
>   care about me.
>
> You are the one who saves me.
>   Please hurry and help!
>
> Psalm 70

Pause and ask yourself...

What emotions are being covered over by my depression? What other feelings do I have:

anger, guilt, hopelessness, resignation? How can I clarify my feelings and be true to my real feelings? What community help can I reach out to in order to help me clarify my feelings?

I feel like a shaky fence...

In the middle of all the emotional confusion and turmoil God can give you inner peace.

> I feel like a shaky fence
> or a sagging wall.
>
> •••
>
> Only God gives inward peace,
> and I depend on him.
> God alone is the mighty rock
> that keeps me safe,
> and he is the fortress
> where I feel secure.
> God saves me and honors me.
> He is that mighty rock
> where I find safety.
>
> Psalm 62. 3a, 5-7

Why am I discouraged?

God cares for you and understands your depression and sadness. With God there is hope. There is always hope in God!

> Why am I discouraged?
> Why am I restless?
> I trust you!
> And I will praise you again
> because you help me,
> and you are my God.
>
> •••
>
> Why am I discouraged?
> Why am I restless?
> I trust you!

And I will praise you again
because you help me,
and you are my God.

Psalm 42. 5, 11

Pause and ask yourself...

How can God and others show me a way to reclaim my life? How can I reclaim my trust and hope again?

"The Lord is all I need; I can depend on him!"

Then I remember something
that fills me with hope.
The LORD's kindness never fails!
If he had not been merciful,
we would have been destroyed.
The LORD can always be trusted
to show mercy each morning.
Deep in my heart I say,
"The LORD is all I need;
I can depend on him!"

Lamentations 3. 21-24

Rebuilding Your Life

"I Will Put My Trust
in the Lord!"

God can be trusted for real help.

Part of rebuilding your life is to put your trust in the Lord's guidance and wisdom. People may sin against you, but God will always treat you with love.

> I praise you, Lord,
>   for being my guide.
> Even in the darkest night,
>   your teachings fill my mind.
> I will always look to you,
> as you stand beside me
>   and protect me from fear.
> With all my heart,
> I will celebrate,
>   and I can safely rest.
>
> • • •
>
> You have shown me
>   the path to life,
> and you make me glad
>   by being near to me.
> Sitting at your right side,
>   I will always be joyful.
>
> Psalm 16. 7-9, 11

Human love may fail you, God's love never fails.

Part of trusting in the Lord is to know that the only totally dependable love in this world is God's love. You can never depend completely on human love, for we all sin against one another. Only God's eternal love endures forever.

What can we say about all this? If God is on our side, can anyone be against us? God did not keep back his own Son, but he gave him for us. If God did this, won't he freely give us everything else? If God says his chosen ones are acceptable to him, can anyone bring charges against them? Or can anyone condemn them? No indeed! Christ died and was raised to life, and now he is at God's right side, speaking to him for us. Can anything separate us from the love of Christ? Can trouble, suffering, and hard times, or hunger and nakedness, or danger and death?
It is exactly as the Scriptures say,

> "For you we face death
>   all day long.
> We are like sheep
> on their way
>   to be butchered."

In everything we have won more than a victory because of Christ who loves us. I am sure that nothing can separate us from God's love — not life or death, not angels or spirits, not the present or the future, and not powers above or powers below. Nothing in all creation can separate us from God's love for us in Christ Jesus our Lord!

Romans 8. 31-39

Pause and ask yourself...

Does the love of my family or friends depend on what I do, or what I don't do? Is it constant or does it change from day to day? What kind of love does God give me?

God wants to rescue you.

Scripture witnesses that God cared for the Israelites and delivered them from slavery in Egypt. Just as God freed the Israelites, God wants to help free you from abuse. You can call on God to fortify you as you boldly press toward safety and truth-telling. Strengthened with God's power, you will be better able to regain control of your life.

The Israelites celebrated their victory from slavery in Egypt in song.

> The LORD is my strength,
> the reason for my song,
>   because he has saved me.
> I praise and honor the LORD —
> he is my God and the God
>   of my ancestors.
>
> • • •
>
> Our LORD, no other gods
> compare with you —
>   Majestic and holy!
>   Fearsome and glorious!
>   Miracle worker!
> When you signaled
>   with your right hand,
> your enemies were swallowed
>   deep into the earth.

> The people you rescued
> were led by your powerful love
> to your holy place.
>
> Exodus 15. 2, 11-13

Pause and ask yourself…

How can God and others help free me from abuse? What actions can I take that will promote my own renewal?

God wants to protect you from harm.

God remains your protector and comforter, even in the midst of abuse. The Lord stands ready to lead you away from every danger into safety.

> I look to the hills!
> Where will I find help?
> It will come from the LORD
> who created the heavens
> and the earth.
>
> The LORD is your protector,
> and he won't go to sleep
> or let you stumble.
> The protector of Israel
> doesn't doze
> or ever get drowsy.
>
> The LORD is your protector,
> there at your right side
> to shade you from the sun.
> You won't be harmed
> by the sun during the day
> or by the moon at night.
>
> The LORD will protect you
> and keep you safe
> from all dangers.

> The Lord will protect you
> now and always
> wherever you go.

>> Psalm 121

Pause and ask yourself...

Can I trust God to be my protector? How can I ask God to intervene on my behalf and to bring me into safety? Can I pray that the Lord will provide others to help me?

God will help you by increasing your endurance and strength.

Abuse can bring on great emotional and physical exhaustion that can sap your strength and erode your will to fight the damage done to you. Against all odds God can renew your strength and hope.

> You people of Israel, say,
> "God pays no attention to us!
>> He doesn't care if we
>> are treated unjustly."

> But how can you say that?
> Don't you know?
>> Haven't you heard?
> The Lord is the eternal God,
>> Creator of the earth.
> He never gets weary or tired;
> his wisdom cannot be measured.

> The Lord gives strength
>> to those who are weary.
> Even young people get tired,
>> then stumble and fall.

> But those who trust the LORD
>   will find new strength.
> They will be strong like eagles
>   soaring upward on wings;
> they will walk and run
>   without getting tired.

>   Isaiah 40. 27-31

Jesus will grant you the strength to overcome any hardship.

The apostle Paul said:

I know what it is to be poor or to have plenty, and I have lived under all kinds of conditions. I know what it means to be full or to be hungry, to have too much or too little. Christ gives me the strength to face anything.

Philippians 4. 12, 13

Pause and ask yourself...

What can I ask of God that will renew my strength? How can I find the inner peace I need to help me move on to new life, even if my situation is not peaceful or even violent?

God will give you spiritual armor to fight against spiritual powers of evil.

Everyone battles against spiritual forces that are not of God, but it is not always easy to know how to wage war against evil. Beware and use the full armor of God as your defense. Strengthen yourself for battle with all the spiritual armor that God has given you: the scriptures, prayer and your devotion to the Lord. When you can find no way out, the Lord can help you find a way. Pray for God's will for the people in your family and for yourself.

Finally, let the mighty strength of the Lord make you strong. Put on all the armor that God gives, so you can defend yourself against the devil's tricks. We are not fighting against humans. We are fighting against forces and authorities and against rulers of darkness and powers in the spiritual world. So put on all the armor that God gives. Then when that evil day comes, you will be able to defend yourself. And when the battle is over, you will still be standing firm.

Be ready! Let the truth be like a belt around your waist, and let God's justice protect you like armor. Your desire to tell the good news about peace should be like shoes on your feet. Let your faith be like a shield, and you will be able to stop all the flaming arrows of the evil one. Let God's saving power be like a helmet, and for a sword use God's message that comes from the Spirit.

Never stop praying, especially for others. Always pray by the power of the Spirit. Stay alert and keep praying for God's people.

Ephesians 6. 10-18

Pause and ask yourself...

How do I put on God's full armor? Do I read the Scriptures and try to practice them in my life? Do I try to live as God would want? Do I recognize that the Lord is mighty and able to help and that others are there to help me?

By the wisdom of God you will be helped to find a solution.

Who can measure the wealth and wisdom and knowledge of God? Who can understand his decisions or explain what he does?

"Has anyone known
the thoughts of the Lord
    or given him advice?"

Romans 11. 33, 34

By prayer you can be open to God's wisdom, and your own wisdom. God may lead you to counter the abuse by calling on others for help and by seeking shelter in a safe place.

In her right hand
    Wisdom holds a long life,
and in her left hand
    are wealth and honor.
Wisdom makes life pleasant
    and leads us safely along.
Wisdom is a life-giving tree,
the source of happiness
    for all who hold on to her.

By his wisdom and knowledge
the Lord created
    heaven and earth.
By his understanding
he let the ocean break loose
    and clouds release the rain.
My child, use common sense
and sound judgment!
    Always keep them in mind.
They will help you to live
    a long and beautiful life.
You will walk safely
    and never stumble;

> you will rest without a worry
> > and sleep soundly.
> So don't be afraid
> > of sudden disasters
> or storms that strike
> > those who are evil.
> You can be sure that the LORD
> > will protect you from harm.

Proverbs 3. 16-26

Pause and ask yourself...

Can I call upon God to strengthen me spiritually and to provide both divine help and physical intervention from qualified professionals, if I am being psychologically tortured, beaten or in a life-threatening situation? If necessary, can I seek advice on when to leave and how? Can I trust God to give me guidance?

God will help to guide you in the right direction.

By praying and surrendering yourself to God's will, you can be open to God's guidance.

> You are my hiding place!
> > You protect me from trouble,
> and you put songs in my heart
> > because you have saved me.
>
> You said to me,
> "I will point out the road
> > that you should follow.
> I will be your teacher
> > and watch over you.

Psalm 32. 7-8

God healed a woman when she took initiative and trusted Jesus.

In the crowd was a woman who had been bleeding for twelve years. She had gone to many doctors, and they had not done anything except cause her a lot of pain. She had paid them all the money she had. But instead of getting better, she only got worse.

The woman had heard about Jesus, so she came up behind him in the crowd and barely touched his clothes. She had said to herself, "If I can just touch his clothes, I will get well." As soon as she touched them, her bleeding stopped, and she knew she was well.

At that moment Jesus felt power go out from him. He turned to the crowd and asked, "Who touched my clothes?"

His disciples said to him, "Look at all these people crowding around you! How can you ask who touched you?" But Jesus turned to see who had touched him.

The woman knew what had happened to her. She came shaking with fear and knelt down in front of Jesus. Then she told him the whole story.

Jesus said to the woman, "You are now well because of your faith. May God give you peace! You are healed, and you will no longer be in pain."

Mark 5. 25-34

God will bless you with the courage to take your own needs seriously. Jesus revealed that God wants to give you every good thing.

Jesus said:

> Suppose one of you goes to a friend in the middle of the night and says, "Let me borrow three loaves of bread. A friend of

mine has dropped in, and I don't have a thing for him to eat." And suppose your friend answers, "Don't bother me! The door is bolted, and my children and I are in bed. I cannot get up to give you something."

He may not get up and give you the bread, just because you are his friend. But he will get up and give you as much as you need, simply because you are not ashamed to keep on asking.

So I tell you to ask and you will receive, search and you will find, knock and the door will be opened for you. Everyone who asks will receive, everyone who searches will find, and the door will be opened for everyone who knocks. Which one of you fathers would give your hungry child a snake if the child asked for a fish? Which one of you would give your child a scorpion if the child asked for an egg? As bad as you are, you still know how to give good gifts to your children. But your heavenly Father is even more ready to give the Holy Spirit to anyone who asks.

Luke 11. 5b-13

Pause and ask yourself...

What is it I want to ask of God to help me rebuild my life?

God always works for the welfare of everyone who loves God.

Even when you are heartsick and hurting God gives you an assurance of a special and eternal hope. The Lord knows your pain and suffering. You can always be confident that God loves and cherishes you, and will provide you relief. God has chosen you for a special purpose. Against all violence, you can be assured that God is always working toward your welfare.

I am sure that what we are suffering now cannot compare with the glory that will be shown to us. In fact, all creation is eagerly waiting for God to show who his children are. Meanwhile, creation is confused, but not because it wants to be confused. God made it this way in the hope that creation would be set free from decay and would share in the glorious freedom of his children. We know that all creation is still groaning and is in pain, like a woman about to give birth.

The Spirit makes us sure about what we will be in the future. But now we groan silently, while we wait for God to show that we are his children. This means that our bodies will also be set free. And this hope is what saves us. But if we already have what we hope for, there is no need to keep on hoping. However, we hope for something we have not yet seen, and we patiently wait for it.

• • •

We know that God is always at work for the good of everyone who loves him. They are the ones God has chosen for his purpose, and he has always known who his chosen ones would be.

Romans 8. 18-25, 28, 29a

Pause and ask yourself...

Can I have the hope that God will work out everything for good? Can I pray that God's chosen purpose for my life be revealed?

Claim the promises that God offers to you.

Jesus said:

> God blesses those people
>   who depend only on him.
> They belong to the kingdom
>   of heaven!
>
> •••
>
> God blesses those people
> who are treated badly
>   for doing right.
> They belong to the kingdom
>   of heaven.

Matthew 5. 3, 10

Pause and ask yourself

How can I claim God's promises for me?

In talking with his disciples Jesus said that sorrow will turn into joy. As you begin to rebuild your life, find hope in Jesus' words and the promise he offers.

When a woman is about to give birth, she is in great pain. But after it is all over, she forgets the pain and is happy, because she has brought a child into the world. You are now very sad. But later I will see you, and you will be so happy that no one will be able to change the way you feel. When that time comes, you won't have to ask me about anything. I tell you for certain that the Father will give you whatever you ask for in my name. You have not asked for anything in this way before, but now you must ask in my name. Then it will be given to you, so that you will be completely happy.

John 16.21-24

Acceptance and Peace

"I Will Praise the Lord!"

You can praise the Lord! Your acceptance of God's gift of life, in abundance, is God's true desire. God promises to bless you as you struggle to heal from the physical and spiritual wounds inflicted upon you. As you walk down the long and difficult road to safety, God will lovingly walk beside you toward new life. God is at work to powerfully strengthen you to trust and receive both God's love and the love of others who have been placed in your life to do God's will against the evil of abuse.

The spiritual gift of inner peace will be yours as you pray for God's guidance and actively seek help in breaking the cycle of abuse and demanding an end to the violence. You will be increasingly favored with the knowledge of God's eternal blessings.

God's love is eternal.

God has unlimited love for you, and freely gives you a surplus of kindness.

> I will praise you, LORD!
>   You saved me from the grave
> and kept my enemies
>   from celebrating my death.

I prayed to you, LORD God,
    and you healed me,
saving me from death
    and the grave.

Your faithful people, LORD,
will praise you with songs
    and honor your holy name.
Your anger lasts a little while,
but your kindness lasts
    for a lifetime.
At night we may cry,
but when morning comes
    we will celebrate.

Psalm 30. 1-5

Pause and ask yourself...

Have I seen changes in my situation? What positive changes have I seen in me: am I more assertive, do I have more confidence? How has God strengthened and supported me?

God's Kingdom is eternal.

Your kingdom will never end,
    and you will rule forever.

Our LORD, you keep your word
    and do everything you say.
When someone stumbles or falls,
    you give a helping hand.
Everyone depends on you,
and when the time is right,
    you provide them with food.
By your own hand you satisfy
    the desires of all who live.

Our LORD, everything you do
    is kind and thoughtful,

and you are near to everyone
> whose prayers are sincere.
You satisfy the desires
> of all your worshipers,
and you come to save them
> when they ask for help.
You take care of everyone
who loves you,
> but you destroy the wicked.

I will praise you, LORD,
and everyone will respect
> your holy name forever.

> Psalm 145. 13-21

Pause and ask yourself...

Can I see the blessings God has given me? Can I see the tender love of the Lord as I rebuild my life?

God's blessings are eternal.

You can praise the wonderful name of the Lord, for you will be crowned with glory and honor for believing in God's promise. Mary was chosen to be the mother of Jesus, and she was blessed because she allowed God's holy purpose to be worked in her life.

Mary said:
> With all my heart
> > I praise the Lord,
> and I am glad
> > because of God my Savior.
> He cares for me,
> > his humble servant.
> From now on,

> all people will say
>> God has blessed me.
> God All-Powerful has done
> great things for me,
>> and his name is holy.
> He always shows mercy
> to everyone
>> who worships him.
> The Lord has used
>> his powerful arm
> to scatter those
>> who are proud.
> He drags strong rulers
>> from their thrones
> and puts humble people
>> in places of power.
> God gives the hungry
>> good things to eat,
> and sends the rich away
>> with nothing.
> He helps his servant Israel
> and is always merciful
>> to his people.
> The Lord made this promise
>> to our ancestors,
> to Abraham and his family
>> forever!

Luke 1. 46-55

God's hope and peace are eternal.

Jesus gives you the precious hope and peace of the Lord.

We have run to God for safety. Now his promises should greatly encourage us to take hold of the hope that is right in front of us. This hope is like a firm and steady anchor for our souls. In fact, hope reaches behind the curtain and into the

most holy place. Jesus has gone there ahead of us,
and he is our high priest forever, just like
Melchizedek.

Hebrews 6. 18b-20

Jesus said:

> I give you peace, the kind of peace that only
> I can give. It isn't like the peace that this
> world can give. So don't be worried or afraid.

John 14. 27

A blessing for you...

> I pray that the LORD
>   will bless and protect you,
> and that he will show you mercy
>   and kindness.
> May the LORD be good to you
>   and give you peace.

Numbers 6. 24-26

SCRIPTURE INDEX

Old Testament

Exodus
15. 2, 11-13 53

Numbers
6. 24-26 68

Deuteronomy
30. 11-17, 19b, 20 20

Job
7. 1-6, 11 18
21. 7, 9, 14-16 36
36. 2b-6 16

Psalms
7. 1-4, 6, 8-11 35
10. 17 7
13. 19
16. 7-9, 11 51
22. 1, 2 25
23 27
25. 1-5 13
27. 1-3, 7-9 25
30. 1-5 64
31. 14-16 12
32. 7, 8 59
35. 22-28 39
38. 6-10 44
42. 1-3 43

42. 5, 11	49
43	47
46. 1-76	22
55. 1-8, 12, 13, 20, 21a	10
62. 3a, 5-7	49
70	48
77. 1-4, 6-9, 11-14	23
97. 6, 10	31
103. 6-8, 11, 12	41
116. 3, 4, 8-11, 15, 16	44
121	54
139. 1-18	30
139. 19-24	37
143. 4-8	46
145. 13-21	65

Proverbs

3. 16-26	58

Isaiah

40. 27-31	55
41. 10-13	27
43. 1-3a	27
49. 15	29

Lamentations

3. 18-20	42
3. 21-24	50

New Testament

Matthew

5. 3, 10	62
6. 9-13	40

11. 28	72
11. 28-30	9
27. 45, 46	24

Mark

5. 25-34	59
11. 15-18	33
12. 28-34	34
14. 43-46	11
15. 16-20	12

Luke

1. 46-55	66
4. 16-21	20
11. 5b-13	59
13. 10-17	32
18. 1-8	40

John

9. 1-7	17
10. 7-10	21
14. 27	68
16. 21-24	63

Romans

8.18-25,28, 29a	61
8. 31-39	52
11. 33, 34	57
12. 19	40

1 Corinthians

| 3. 16, 17 | 14 |
| 6. 19, 20 | 33 |

Ephesians
1. 3-10 15
6. 10-18 56

Philippians
4. 12, 13 56

Hebrews
6. 18b-20 67

1 Peter
1. 19-22a 14

Jesus said,

> *If you are tired from carrying heavy burdens,
> come to me and I will give you rest.*

Matthew 11. 28